CONTINENTS

Australia

Mary Virginia Fox

Heinemann Library
Chicago, Illinois

© 2001 Reed Educational & Professional Publishing
Published by Heinemann Library,
an imprint of Reed Educational & Professional Publishing,
Chicago, IL

Customer Service 888-454-2279

Visit our website at www.heinemannlibrary.com

Designed by Depke Design
Printed in Hong Kong

05 04 03 02
10 9 8 7 6 5 4 3 2

Library of Congress Catalog–in–Publication Data
Fox, Mary Virginia.
     Australia / Mary Virginia Fox.
        p. cm. -- (Continents)
     Includes bibliographical references (p.) and index.
     ISBN 1-57572-449-9 (lib. bdg.)   ISBN 1-58810-948-8 (pbk. bdg.)
     1. Australia--Juvenile literature. [1. Australia.] I. Title. II. Continents

(Chicago, Ill.)
DU96 .F7 2001
994--dc21   00-011467

Acknowledgments
The publishers are grateful to the following for permission to reproduce copyright material: Earth Scenes/Dani/Jeske, pp. 5, 17; Earth Scenes/Michael Fogden, p. 6; Bruce Coleman/Eric Crichton, p. 8, 21; Peter Arnold/J.P. Perrero, p. 12; Bruce Coleman, Inc./Norman Owen Tomalin, p. 14, 20; Bruce Coleman, Inc./Hans Reinhard, p. 16; Animals Animals/Hans & Judy Beste, p. 15; Peter Arnold/John Cancalosi, p. 19; Photo Researchers/Georg Gerster, p. 22; Bruce Coleman, Inc./Bob Burch, p. 26; Earth Scenes/Paddy Ryan, p.11; Tony Stone/Robin Smith, p. 24; Photo Researchers/Bill Buchman, p. 25; Tony Stone/Doug Armand, p. 27; Photo Researchers/A. Flowers & L. Newman, p. 28.

Every effort has been made to contact copyright holders of any material reproduced in this book.

Any omissions will be rectified in subsequent printings if notice is given to the publisher.

Some words are shown in bold, **like this.** You can find out what they mean by looking in the glossary.

Contents

Where Is Australia? 4

Weather 6

Mountains 8

Rivers 10

Lakes 12

Animals 14

Plants 16

Languages 18

Cities 20

In the Country 24

Famous Places 26

Fast Facts 30

Glossary 31

More Books to Read 32

Index 32

Where Is Australia?

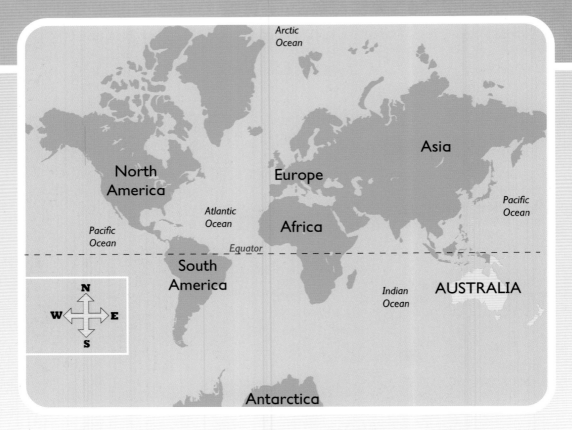

There are seven continents in the world. Australia is the smallest. It is located in the **Southern Hemisphere.** Australia is also a country that takes up the whole continent.

Great Australian Bight, South Australia

Australia is surrounded by water. To the east is the South Pacific Ocean. The southern Indian Ocean splashes Australia's southern coast.

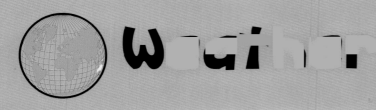
Weather

Everlasting Daisies Outback, New South Wales

The north of Australia is close to the **equator**. It is wet and hot there. Swamps and **rain forests** cover much of this area. Dry deserts take up the middle of Australia.

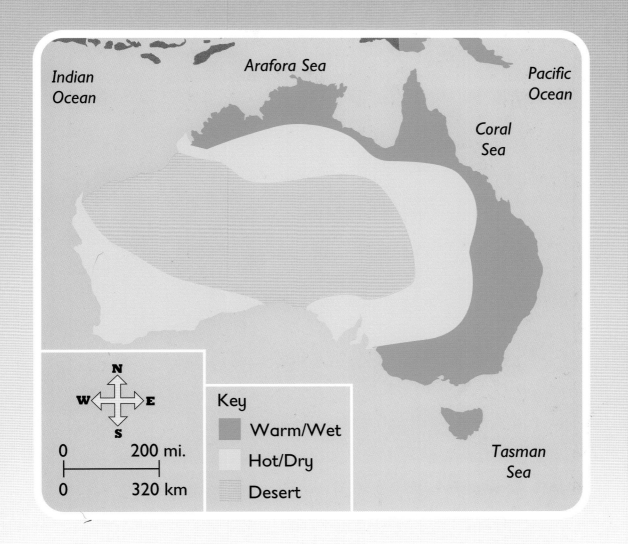

Because Australia is in the **Southern Hemisphere,** the seasons are opposite those in the **Northern Hemisphere.** Winter lasts from June to September, which is summertime in the United States.

Mountains

Mount Kosciusko

Australia is the flattest of all the continents. Rain and wind have worn away the **ancient** mountains. The highest mountain in Australia is Mount Kosciusko.

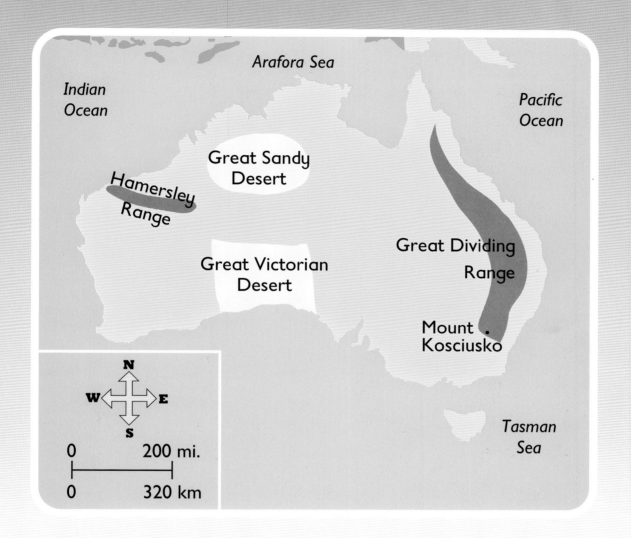

There are two mountain **ranges** in Australia. The Great Dividing Range sits on part of the east **coast.** The Hamersly Range cuts across the northwest of Australia.

Rivers

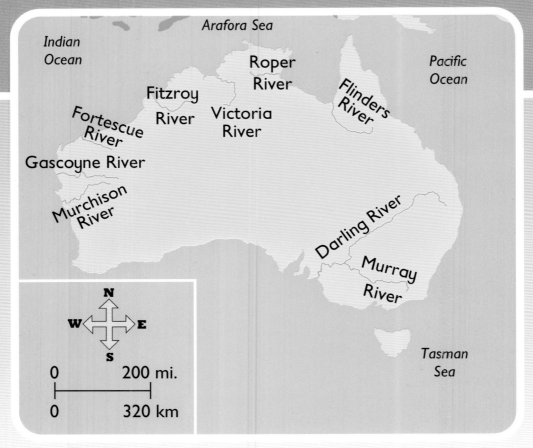

Indian Ocean

Arafora Sea

Pacific Ocean

Roper River

Fitzroy River

Fortescue River

Victoria River

Flinders River

Gascoyne River

Murchison River

Darling River

Murray River

N
W E
S

0   200 mi.

0   320 km

Tasman Sea

Some rivers are short and fast. Many flow from the Great Dividing **Range** into the ocean. Water from the Darling River is used to grow **crops**.

Murray and Darling Rivers

The Murray River is the longest river that flows all year. Many of Australia's rivers are dry part of the year.

Lakes

Lake Eyre

Lake Eyre is the largest lake in Australia. It is also the lowest point on the continent. **Tourists** visit and camp in a large park that surrounds the lake.

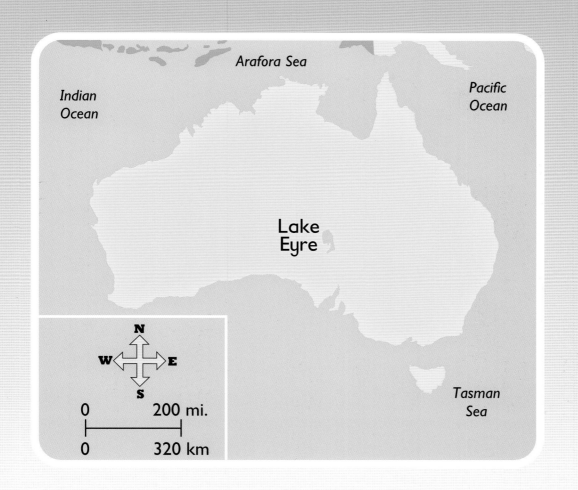

Australia has many small lakes. These lakes are dry for much of the year. Some are filled with water only in the rainy season. These dry **lake beds** are covered with salt and clay.

Animals

Emu

Some birds that live in Australia cannot fly. The emu is a very large bird. An emu can be as tall as an adult person. The cassowary has long skinny legs, which it uses to run very fast.

kangaroo and baby, or joey

Animals such as the kangaroo and the koala live only in Australia. The mothers of these animals carry their babies in their **pouches**.

Plants

Eucalyptus trees

Eucalyptus trees grow in all kinds of **soil** and can be very tall. There are more than 500 kinds of eucalyptus trees in Australia.

Kangaroo paw

Wild flowers, like the kangaroo paw, grow only during the rainy season. They are very colorful. Some are shaped like the hind foot of a kangaroo.

Aboriginal children

The first people to live in Australia are called **aborigines.** At one time, there were many **tribes** that moved from place to place to find food. Each tribe spoke its own language.

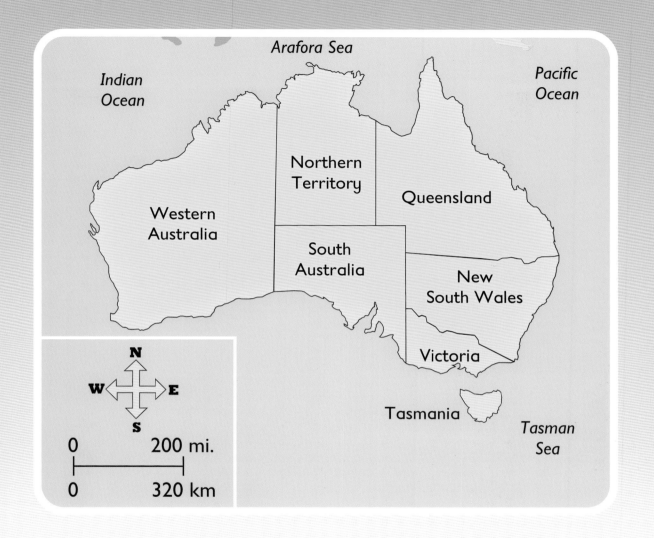

The country of Australia takes up the whole continent. People from England sailed to Australia over 200 years ago. They brought their language with them. Today, most people in Australia speak English.

Cities

Home in New South Wales

Most Australians live in cities along the **coasts.**
Many people live in homes that have lawns and
gardens. With such warm weather, Australians
like to spend their time outdoors.

Melbourne, Australia

Sydney and Melbourne are the largest cities in Australia. Hotels and **skyscrapers** tower above the busy city streets.

Perth, Western Australia

Perth is the largest city on Australia's west **coast.** It has many factories. **Tourists** come to visit Perth's sandy beaches and museums.

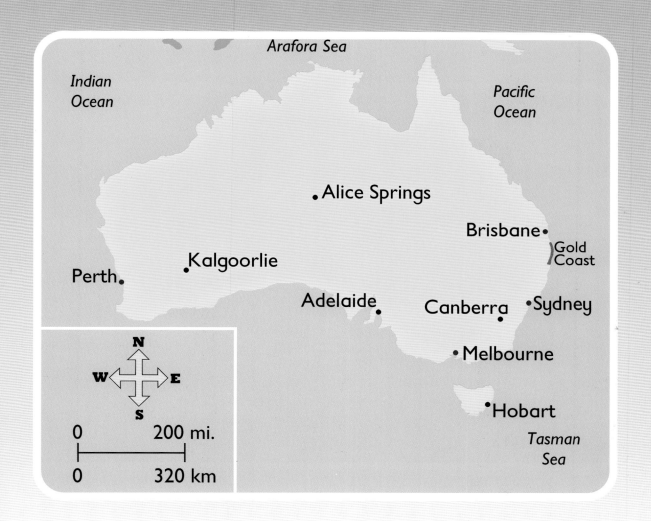

Most Australian cities are on the coasts. There are many **harbors** and beautiful beaches. The area south of Brisbane is called the Gold Coast. Many fancy hotels have been built here.

Northern Territory

The **outback** is the big middle area of Australia. **Cattle** and sheep farmers live on **ranches.** Towns and neighbors are usually very far apart.

School of the Air, Northern Territory

Many children in the outback learn their school lessons by listening to a radio or using a computer. Some doctors must fly in airplanes to see their **patients**.

Sydney Opera House

The Sydney **Opera** House sits on the **shore** of Sydney **Harbor.** The strange roof makes this building one of the most famous in the world.

Ayers Rock, Uluru National Park, central Australia

Ayers Rock is a large red mountain of rock in the middle of the **outback**. It is a **sacred** place for the **aborigines**. These people have lived in Australia for more than 30,000 years.

Great Barrier Reef

Off the east **coast** is the Great Barrier Reef. It is the world's largest **coral reef.** People from around the world come here to swim and see the many fish and beautiful coral.

The Trans-Australian Railway runs straight through the **outback.** Before it was built, people had to walk across the desert or ride on camels.

1. Australia is the only country that is also a continent.

2. The official name of Australia is "Commonwealth of Australia."

3. Australia has six states: New South Wales, Queensland, South Australia, Tasmania, Victoria, and Western Australia.

4. Towns in the outback can be 100 miles (160 kilometers) apart.

5. A popular outdoor activity is camel racing.

6. Because Australia is surrounded by water, some call it the "island continent."

7. The Great Barrier Reef is the world's largest coral reef.

Glossary

aborigine one of the first people to live in Australia

ancient something from a very long time ago

cattle cows, bulls, steers, and oxen

coast land right next to water

coral reef underwater rocklike forms made up of the skeletons of tiny sea animals

crop farm product grown in soil

equator imaginary circle around the exact middle of the earth

harbor safe place for ships and boats to stay

lake bed ground beneath a lake

Northern Hemisphere half of the earth north of the equator

opera play with music in which all or most of the words are sung

outback large grassland and desert area in the middle of Australia

patient person a doctor or dentist takes care of

pouch bag or sacklike part of some animals in which babies are carried

rain forest thick forest that gets heavy rainfall all year

ranch very large farm on which animals are raised, usually cattle or sheep

range line of connected mountains

sacred something treated with great honor and respect

shore land next to a body of water

soil dirt in which plants grow

Southern Hemisphere half of the earth south of the equator

tourist person visiting a place for fun

tribe group of people or families living together with the same leader or chief

More Books to Read

McCollum, Sean. *Australia.* Minneapolis, Minn.: Lerner Publishing Group, 1999.

Bell, Rachael. *Australia.* Chicago: Heinemann Library, 1999.

Index

aborigines 18, 27
Africa 4
animals 14–15
cities 20–23
country 24–25
England 19
equator 6
famous places 26–29
Indian Ocean 5
lakes 12–13
languages 18–19
mountains 8–9
Mount Kosciusko 8

New South Wales 6, 20
Northern Hemisphere 7
Northern Territory 24, 25
outback 6, 24, 27, 29
plants 16–17
rivers 10–11
school 25
Southern Hemisphere 4, 7
South America 4
South Pacific Ocean 5
United States 7
weather 6–7